Look at the picture of this park.

Can you see a boat and a duck on the pond?
And a fish?

Can you find a bird, a tree and flowers?
Can you see a butterfly and a ladybird?

Draw the boat. Draw a rectangle.
Put two triangles on it and a square.

triangle

rectangle

I can draw a boat.

Look! The fish is swimming.
Draw an oval body with a triangle on it.
Draw a triangle for the tail.

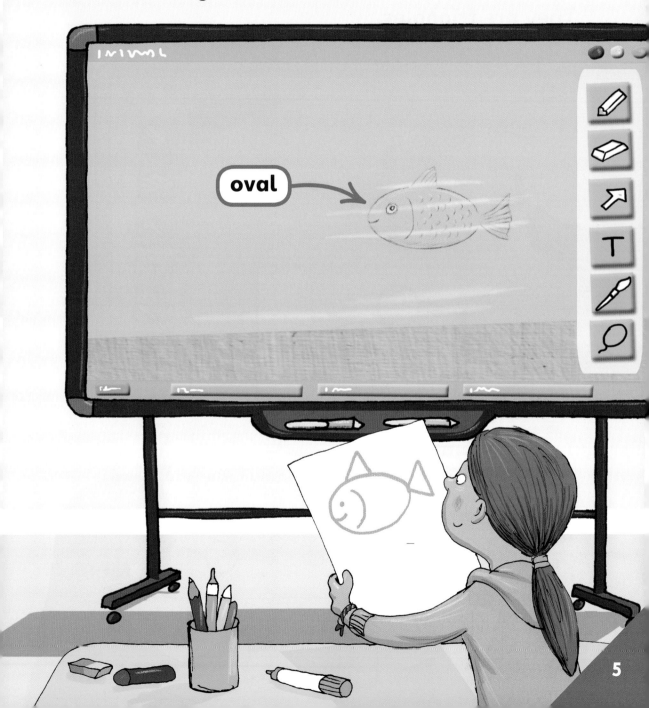

oval

Look at the duck.
Draw two ovals and a circle.
Now draw the tail and the beak.
They are triangles.

Draw the bird.
Draw oval wings and triangles
for its tail and beak.

Look at all the flowers.
Draw yellow circles and red ovals.
Now draw curved leaves.

The flowers are small but the tree is tall.
Draw a straight tree with oval leaves.
Its seeds are circles.

Look at the red ladybird. Draw its body.
Draw a curved line and black circles.

Look at this beautiful butterfly.
Draw its blue body and wings.
Put straight lines and small ovals on its wings.

13

drawings

Now look at these famous pictures and drawings.
There are many shapes in them.
Artists can draw and we can draw.

Activities

Before You Read

1 Match the shapes with the words.

a square   **b** triangle   **c** rectangle   **d** circle   **e** oval

After You Read

1 Look at the four drawings. What shapes can you see?
What lines can you see?

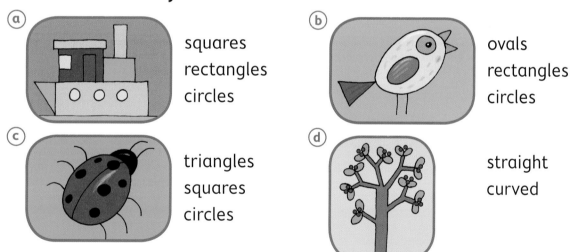

a squares
rectangles
circles

b ovals
rectangles
circles

c triangles
squares
circles

d straight
curved

2 Draw this garden in your notebook.
The garden has got a tree and six yellow flowers.
There is a bird on the tree.
There is a ladybird on a flower.
There are two blue butterflies.

Pearson Education Limited
Edinburgh Gate, Harlow,
Essex CM20 2JE, England
and Associated Companies throughout the world.

ISBN: 978-1-4082-8826-9

This edition first published by Pearson Education Ltd 2014
7 9 10 8 6
Text copyright © Pearson Education Ltd 2014

The moral rights of the author have been asserted
in accordance with the Copyright Designs and Patents Act 1988

Set in 19/23pt OT Fiendstar Semibold
Printed in China
SWTC/06

Acknowledgements
The publisher would like to thank the following for their kind permission to reproduce their photographs:
(Key: b-bottom; c-centre; l-left; r-right; t-top)

14 Bridgeman Art Library Ltd: Giraudon (tl). **Fotolia.com:** ottoflick (bl); magnia (br); ARK (tr)

All other images © Pearson Education

Every effort has been made to trace the copyright holders and we apologise in advance
for any unintentional omissions. We would be pleased to insert the appropriate
acknowledgement in any subsequent edition of this publication.

Illustrations: Andrew Rowland (Advocate)

Published by Pearson Education Ltd.

For a complete list of the titles available in the Pearson English Kids Readers series, please go to
www.pearsonenglishkidsreaders.com. Alternatively, write to your local Pearson Education office or to
Pearson English Readers Marketing Department, Pearson Education, Edinburgh Gate, Harlow, Essex CM202JE, England.